SUPER SIMPLE MAKERSPACE STEAM CHALLENGE

CONSTRUCT A TINY HOUSE!

And More Architecture Challenges

Megan Borgert-Spaniol

Consulting Editor, Diane Craig,
M.A./Reading Specialist

Super Sandcastle

An Imprint of Abdo Publishing
abdobooks.com

abdobooks.com

Published by Abdo Publishing, a division of ABDO, PO Box 398166, Minneapolis, Minnesota 55439. Copyright © 2021 by Abdo Consulting Group, Inc. International copyrights reserved in all countries. No part of this book may be reproduced in any form without written permission from the publisher. Super SandCastle™ is a trademark and logo of Abdo Publishing.

Printed in the United States of America, North Mankato, Minnesota
102020
012021

Design: Kelly Doudna, Mighty Media, Inc.
Production: Mighty Media, Inc.
Editor: Liz Salzmann
Cover Photographs: Mighty Media, Inc.; Shutterstock Images (girl)
Interior Photographs: Dmitry Ternovoy/Wikimedia Commons, p. 6 (Hadid); Eurleif/Wikimedia Commons, p. 25 (K'NEX bridge); Karel Bartik/Shutterstock Images, p. 24 (sociable weaver bird); Mighty Media, Inc., pp. 10, 11, 15, 16, 17, 18, 19, 20, 21, 22, 26, 27, 28, 29; Shutterstock Images, pp. 4, 6, 7, 9, 10 (plastic, playing cards), 11 (plastic, playing cards), 12, 13, 23, 24, 25, 28 (boy), 30
Design Elements: Mighty Media, Inc.; Shutterstock Images

The following manufacturer/name appearing in this book is a trademark:
Mod Podge®

Library of Congress Control Number: 2020940266

Publisher's Cataloging-in-Publication Data

Names: Borgert-Spaniol, Megan, author.
Title: Construct a tiny house! and more architecture challenges / by Megan Borgert-Spaniol
Description: Minneapolis, Minnesota : Abdo Publishing, 2021 | Series: Super simple makerspace STEAM challenge
Identifiers: ISBN 9781532194351 (lib. bdg.) | ISBN 9781098213718 (ebook)
Subjects: LCSH: Handicraft for children--Juvenile literature. | Building--Juvenile literature. | Architecture--Juvenile literature. | Architectural engineering—Juvenile literature. | Small houses--Juvenile literature.
Classification: DDC 745.5--dc23

Super SandCastle™ books are created by a team of professional educators, reading specialists, and content developers around five essential components—phonemic awareness, phonics, vocabulary, text comprehension, and fluency—to assist young readers as they develop reading skills and strategies and increase their general knowledge. All books are written, reviewed, and leveled for guided reading and early reading intervention programs for use in shared, guided, and independent reading and writing activities to support a balanced approach to literacy instruction.

TO ADULT HELPERS

The challenges in this book can be done using common crafting materials and household items. To keep kids safe, provide assistance with sharp or hot objects. Be sure to protect clothing and work surfaces from messy supplies. Be ready to offer guidance during brainstorming and assist when necessary.

CONTENTS

Become a Maker — 4
Challenge: Architecture — 6
Challenge Extended — 8
Gather Your Materials — 10
Real Architects, Real Challenges — 12
Challenge Accepted! — 14
Challenge 1: Perfect Playground — 15
Challenge 2: Animal-Inspired Stadium — 17
Challenge 3: Pleasant Pavilion — 19
Challenge 4: Hound Home — 21
How Did You Do? — 23
Get Inspired — 24
Helpful Hacks — 26
Problem-Solving — 28
A New Day, A New Challenge — 30
Glossary — 32

BECOME A MAKER

A makerspace is like a laboratory. It's a place where ideas are formed and problems are solved. Kids like you create amazing things in makerspaces. Many makerspaces are in schools and libraries. But they can also be in kitchens, bedrooms, and backyards. Anywhere can be a makerspace when you use imagination, inspiration, **collaboration**, and problem-solving!

IMAGINATION

This takes you to new places and lets you experience new things. Anything is possible with imagination!

INSPIRATION

This is the spark that gives you an idea. Inspiration can come from almost anywhere!

Makerspace Toolbox

COLLABORATION

Makers work together. They ask questions and get ideas from everyone around them. **Collaboration** solves problems that seem impossible.

PROBLEM-SOLVING

Things often don't go as planned when you're creating. But that's part of the fun! Find creative **solutions** to any problem that comes up. These will make your project even better.

CHALLENGE: ARCHITECTURE

Think of all the buildings you enter each day. You probably spend most of your time at your school or in your home. But what about your local library, shopping mall, or movie theater? When you enter any building, you are interacting with architecture.

Architecture is the art and science of **designing** and building structures. People who practice architecture are called architects. Architects face challenges every day.

MEET AN ARCHITECT

Zaha Hadid was born in Iraq in 1950. She later moved to London, where she became an architect. Many of her buildings feature curves or sharp angles. Hadid won many awards for the buildings she designed around the world.

ELI AND EDYTHE BROAD ART MUSEUM, MICHIGAN

Architects build houses, apartment buildings, and other **residential** spaces.

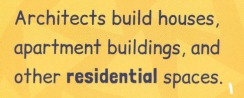

Architects construct museums, libraries, train stations, and other public buildings.

Architects **design** parks, city plazas, and other outdoor spaces for people to enjoy.

CHALLENGE EXTENDED

Architects are challenged by demands. Demands are needs or desires that must be met. Architects are also challenged by limits. These might be time limits or space limits. Architects might also be limited by what materials they can use. The key is figuring out how to meet demands while working within any limits.

Are you ready to be an architect in your makerspace? Read on to find out how the challenges in this book work!

HOW IT WORKS

There are four challenges in this book. Each challenge presents a task to complete.

The task will come with at least one demand or limit. That's what makes it a challenge!

Each challenge will have more difficult demands and limits than the last. That's why it's a good idea to start with Challenge 1 and work up to Challenge 4.

More Minds

Invite others to tackle these challenges with you! You can work together as a group. Or, you can work individually and compare results.

GATHER YOUR MATERIALS

There are a few materials you'll need to do the architecture challenges in this book.

STOPWATCH

FLAT CARDBOARD SQUARES

PLAYING CARDS

IMAGINE

IT'S UP TO YOU WHAT ADDITIONAL MATERIALS YOU USE. EVERY MAKERSPACE HAS DIFFERENT SUPPLIES. WHAT'S IN YOUR SPACE? GATHER MATERIALS THAT YOU CAN USE FOR STRUCTURE, CONNECTING, AND DECORATION.

STRUCTURE

These materials provide your creation with shape and support.

BOARD

ALUMINUM PAN

PLASTIC BAGS

CONNECTING
These materials help connect the different parts of your creation.

DECORATIONS & DETAILS
These materials add fun **details** that make your creation stand out.

11

REAL ARCHITECTS, REAL CHALLENGES

Before you take on your architecture challenges, get inspired! Start by discovering some real-world challenges that architects have faced. Check out the amazing results of these challenges!

CHALLENGE: **DESIGN** BUILDINGS THAT COMBINE LIVING AND SOCIAL SPACES WITH NATURAL SPACES.

RESULT: THE INTERLACE, AN APARTMENT **COMPLEX** IN SINGAPORE. ITS MANY BUILDINGS ARE **STACKED** LIKE BLOCKS AND SURROUNDED BY **RECREATIONAL** SPACES.

CHALLENGE: TURN AN ELEVATED RAILWAY IN NEW YORK CITY INTO A BEAUTIFUL PUBLIC PARK.

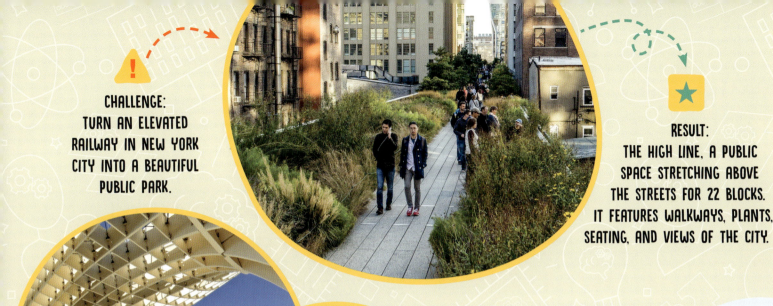

RESULT: THE HIGH LINE, A PUBLIC SPACE STRETCHING ABOVE THE STREETS FOR 22 BLOCKS. IT FEATURES WALKWAYS, PLANTS, SEATING, AND VIEWS OF THE CITY.

CHALLENGE: **DESIGN** A STRUCTURE TO MAKE A PUBLIC AREA IN SEVILLE, SPAIN, MORE INTERESTING.

RESULT: THE METROPOL PARASOL, A WOODEN STRUCTURE WITH SIX MUSHROOMLIKE **CANOPIES**. VISITORS CAN VIEW THE CITY FROM A WALKWAY ON TOP OF THE CANOPIES!

IMAGINE

CAN YOU THINK OF OTHER POSSIBLE **SOLUTIONS** TO THESE CHALLENGES? WHAT IS THE WILDEST IDEA YOU CAN COME UP WITH?

CHALLENGE ACCEPTED!

HERE'S SOME ADVICE FOR TACKLING THE CHALLENGES IN THIS BOOK:

1. **LOOK BEYOND THE MAKERSPACE.** The perfect material might be in your garage, kitchen, or toy chest.

2. **ASK FOR HELP.** Share ideas with friends and family. Ask them for their ideas. Starting with many minds can lead you to places you'd never go on your own!

3. **THINK IT THROUGH.** Don't give up when things don't go exactly as planned. Instead, think about the problem you are having. What are some ways to solve it?

4. **BE CONFIDENT.** You may not know right away how you'll meet a challenge. But trust that you will come up with a **solution**. Start every challenge by saying, "Challenge Accepted!"

Do you have the materials you need? Are you inspired by the work of architects? Then read on for your first challenge!

CHALLENGE 1:
PERFECT PLAYGROUND

TASK: Build a model of your dream playground.

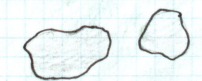

DEMAND
The playground must include the following elements:
- At least three levels
- At least one slide
- At least one climbing structure

LIMIT
The model must fit on a surface that is 18 inches (45 cm) square.

16

CHALLENGE 2:
ANIMAL-INSPIRED STADIUM

TASK: Build a model for a sports **stadium**.

bowerbird nest

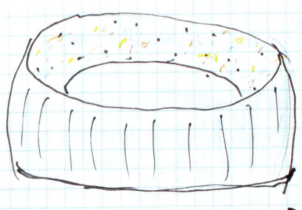

Sports Stadium

DEMAND
The stadium's **design** must be inspired by an animal's home. This could be a bird's nest, beehive, beaver lodge, or other animal home.

LIMIT
You must complete the model in 60 minutes or less.

17

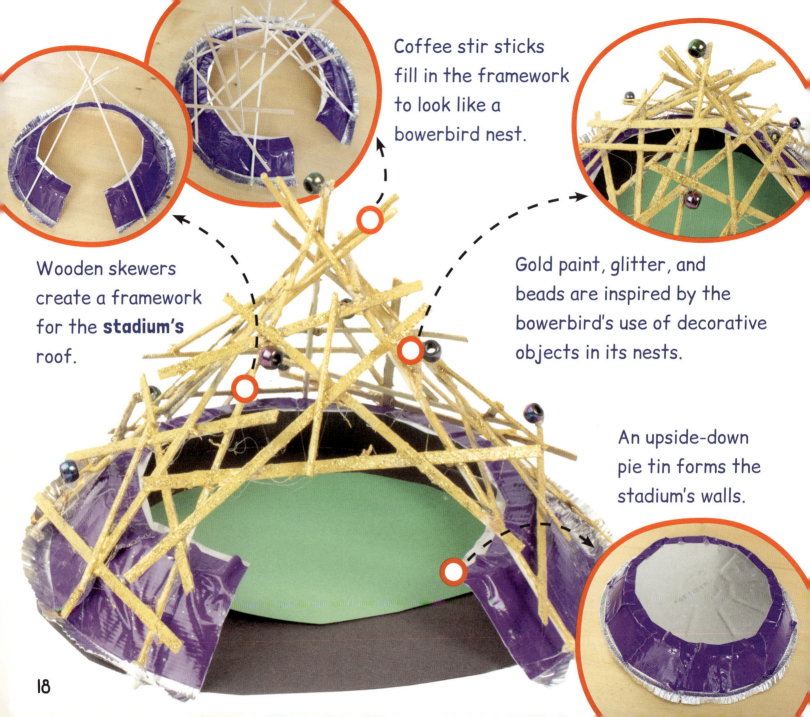

Coffee stir sticks fill in the framework to look like a bowerbird nest.

Gold paint, glitter, and beads are inspired by the bowerbird's use of decorative objects in its nests.

Wooden skewers create a framework for the **stadium's** roof.

An upside-down pie tin forms the stadium's walls.

CHALLENGE 3:
PLEASANT PAVILION

TASK: Design a model of a pavilion. This is an open structure that provides shelter in public spaces.

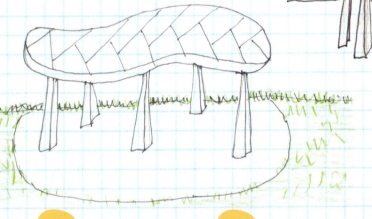

✓ **DEMAND**
The pavilion must provide shelter from rain.

✓ **DEMAND**
The pavilion must be open to the outdoors.

✓ **DEMAND**
The pavilion must be **asymmetrical**.

❌ **LIMIT**
You may use no more than three structural materials and three connecting materials. You may use any number of decorative materials.

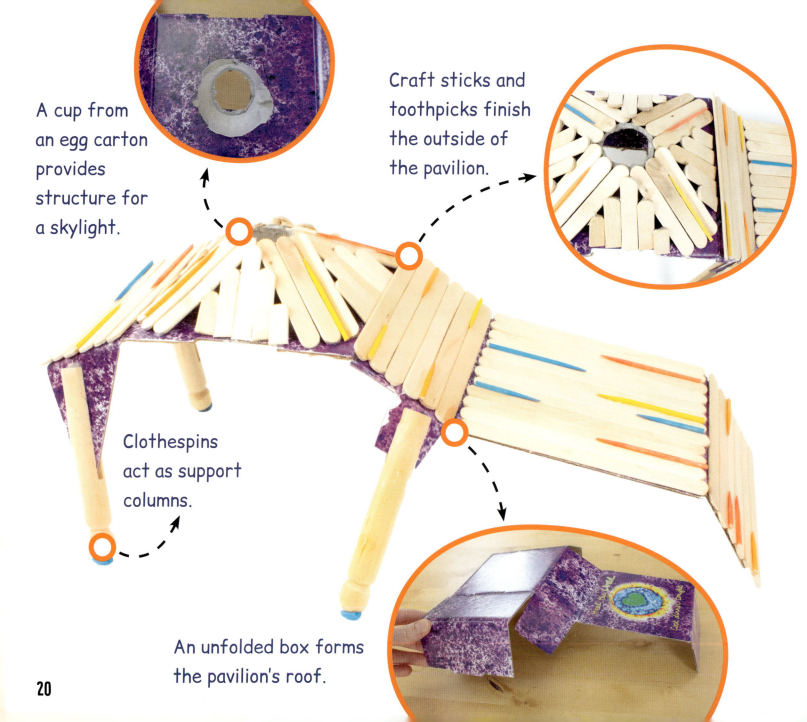

A cup from an egg carton provides structure for a skylight.

Craft sticks and toothpicks finish the outside of the pavilion.

Clothespins act as support columns.

An unfolded box forms the pavilion's roof.

CHALLENGE 4:
HOUND HOME

TASK: Build a tiny, temporary house for a dog.

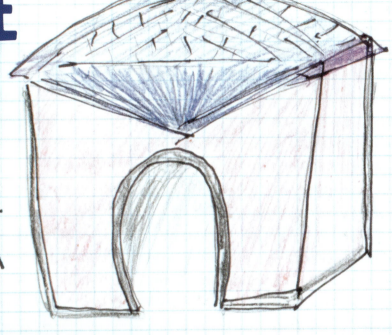

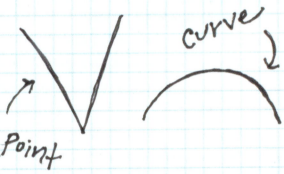

✓ DEMAND
The house must be large enough for a dog to comfortably enter, lie down inside, and exit. You can decide whether the house is for a small or large dog.

✓ DEMAND
The structure must include curves or sharp angles or both.

✗ LIMIT
The tiny house must be made of weatherproof materials so it can be used outside.

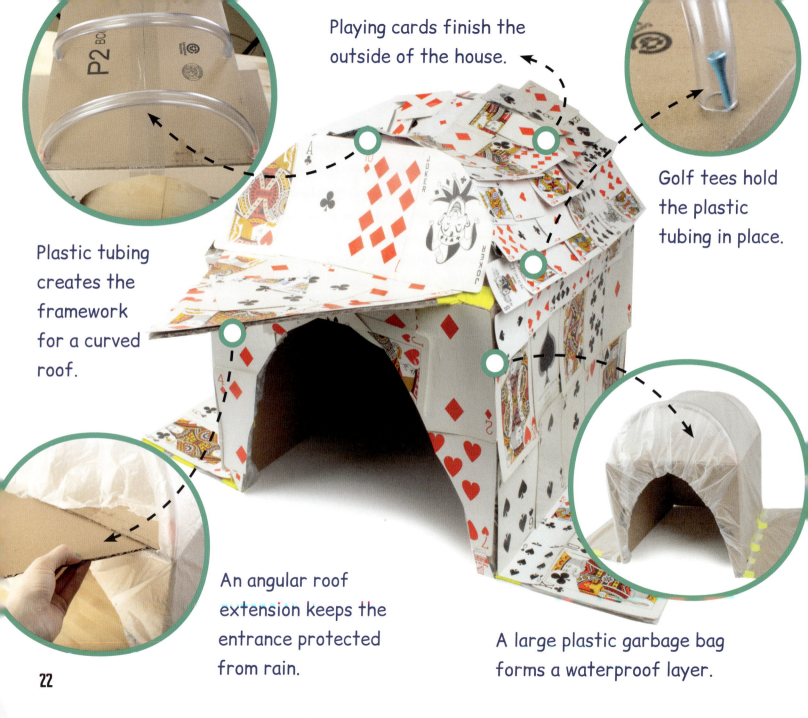

Playing cards finish the outside of the house.

Golf tees hold the plastic tubing in place.

Plastic tubing creates the framework for a curved roof.

An angular roof extension keeps the entrance protected from rain.

A large plastic garbage bag forms a waterproof layer.

22

HOW DID YOU DO?

After you've completed each challenge, think about how it went.

WHAT IS ANOTHER WAY YOU COULD HAVE APPROACHED THE SAME CHALLENGE?

WHAT WAS THE MOST DIFFICULT PART OF THE CHALLENGE?

WHAT WOULD HAVE MADE THE TASK EASIER?

WHAT KINDS OF PROBLEMS CAME UP, AND HOW DID YOU SOLVE THEM?

GET INSPIRED

As a makerspace architect, you can find inspiration nearly anywhere. This will help you approach your challenges with a ton of ideas!

LOOK AT NATURE

Animals are expert architects. Beavers create cozy river lodges using sticks and mud. Honeybees build honeycomb out of wax from their bodies. Sociable weaver birds construct giant nests with dozens of small rooms inside!

LOOK AT PUBLIC SPACES

Next time you are out in your town, take note of the public spaces. These include plazas, walkways, and gardens. Look for any seating, stairs, lighting, and natural features. Notice how people interact with these elements. These are things that architects think about when they are planning spaces.

LOOK AT TOYS

Have you ever played with Lincoln Logs, LEGO bricks, or K'NEX? You can learn a lot about architecture by playing with toy construction sets like these. You can also create your own building units inspired by the ones in these sets.

25

HELPFUL HACKS

As you work, you might discover ways to make challenging tasks easier. Keep these simple tricks and **techniques** in mind as you work through your architecture challenges.

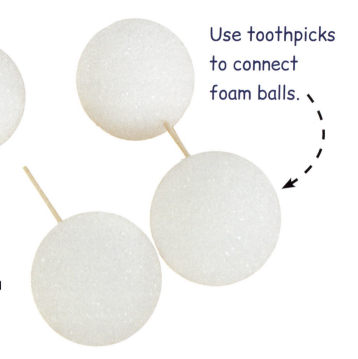

Use toothpicks to connect foam balls.

Mod Podge gives objects a water-resistant finish.

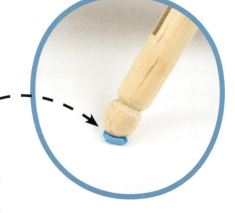

Poster putty is a good way to keep a model from sliding.

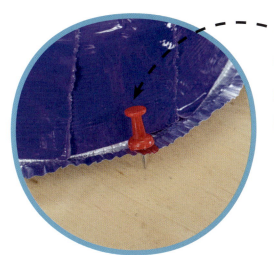

When poking holes in a sturdy material, first make a starter hole with a pushpin.

Carefully use tin snips to easily trim wooden skewers.

Create tree leaves by wrapping small squares of tissue paper around the eraser end of a pencil. Then dip the leaves in glue and press them to the surface you want to cover.

27

PROBLEM-SOLVING

You'll probably run into problems as you attempt the challenges in this book. Instead of giving up, open your mind to new ideas. You'll likely find more than one **solution** to your problem!

PROBLEM
The clothespin branches on your playground tree can't support much weight.

THINK
Why is this happening? Maybe their connection to the tree trunk isn't sturdy enough.

BRAINSTORM AND TEST

Try coming up with three possible **solutions** to any problem. Maybe your tiny house isn't heavy enough and gets blown over by the wind. You could:

1. Place a few heavy items inside the house to weigh it down.

2. Use stakes and rope to fasten the house to the ground.

3. Build a wind barrier around your tiny house using large rocks and sticks.

SOLUTION

Push a skewer through the tree to make a support beam. Connect the clothespin branches to the beam.

A NEW DAY, A NEW CHALLENGE

If you had trouble meeting a challenge, try it again another day with fresh ideas. And if you did meet a challenge, still try it again! There is always more than one way to do something. Give yourself new demands and limits to give the task a new twist.

BEYOND THE MAKERSPACE

You can use your makerspace toolbox to take on everyday challenges, such as building a snowperson or constructing a fort. But architects use the same toolbox to do big things. One day, these tools could help create underwater homes or walkways in the sky. Turn your world into a makerspace challenge! What problems could you solve?

GLOSSARY

asymmetrical – having two sides or halves that are not the same.

canopy – a protective covering, such as an awning or high, leafy branches.

collaboration – the act of working with another person or group in order to do something or reach a goal.

complex – a building or a group of buildings with related units.

design – to plan how something will appear or work. A design is a sketch or outline of something that will be made.

detail – a small part of something.

recreational – used for relaxing or having fun.

residential – related to structures where people live.

solution – an answer to, or a way to solve, a problem.

stacked – to be arranged in a pile.

stadium – a large building with an open area for sporting events surrounded by rows of seats.

technique – a method or style in which something is done.